FANMI MWEN

My Family

Written by Carline Smothers

Illustrations by Fuuji Takashi

Paran mwen te fèt an Ayiti. Sa a se manman m'.

My parents were born in Haiti. This is my mother.

Sa a se papa m'.

This is my father.

Sa yo se sè m' ak frè m.

This is my sister and my brother.

Sa a se matant mwen.

This is my auntie.

Sa a se tonton mwen.

This is my uncle.

Sa a se grann mwen.

This is my grandma.

Fanmi mwen!

My family!

FAMILY

Ki moun ki nan fanmi ou?

Mother

Sisters

Grandma

Grandpa

Aunties

Uncles

Cousins

TREE

Who's in your family?

Brothers

Father

Grandpa

Grandma

Uncles

Aunties

Cousins

Message to reader...

Love yourself for who you are, and be proud of where you've come from.